SCHOOLING PRINCIPLES

by

Michael J. Stevens

Illustrations by

Carole Vincer

KENILWORTH PRESS

First published in the UK in 1997
by Kenilworth Press, an imprint of Quiller Publishing Ltd

Reprinted 1999, 2004, 2008

British Library Cataloguing-in-Publication Data
A catalogue record for this book
is available from the British Library

ISBN 978 1 872082 95 0

Printed in China

Kenilworth Press

An imprint of Quiller Publishing Ltd
Wykey House, Wykey, Shrewsbury, SY4 1JA
Tel: 01939 261616 Fax: 01939 261606
E-mail: info@quillerbooks.com
Website: www.kenilworthpress.com

CONTENTS

SCHOOLING
PRINCIPLES

4 Introduction
5 Handling and Training
8 Relaxation
10 Balance
13 Regularity
14 Energy and Impulsion
16 Bending and Suppleness
18 Straightness
19 Contact
22 Collection
24 Three Stages of Training

Introduction

Watch a group of horses at liberty and you will see peaceful animals moving about majestically as Mother Nature intended. Take one of these noble creatures and set a rider upon his back, and straight away he is unable to exercise his free will. He is prevented from reacting naturally to the influences of the environment, and is constrained instead to move as and when his rider directs. Very often all grace and facility of movement are lost in an instant.

How can we restore to the ridden horse the beauty that nature bestows upon him when he is free? This is the question that lies at the very heart of the art of riding. Answer this and you know everything. Every true horseman must embark upon a pilgrimage to seek the answer, for therein lies the quintessential secret of horsemanship.

The Rider's Seat

Above all, the rider must realise that a major effect of his presence on the back of a horse is to interfere with the natural posture, balance, and movement of his mount. In order to minimise this encumbrance the rider must know how to sit: without a seat that enables him to move as one with his horse, he will never have much success at schooling the horse.

A Training Method

The horse has played such an important part in the history of civilisation, that over the centuries a very successful method of preparing and training him under the saddle has evolved. *Classical riding,* as it is now known, aims not merely to restore natural posture and movement to the ridden horse, but also to improve upon them.

Although we commonly speak of 'training' horses, we do not mean that they are drilled to respond to a set of signals. Instead they are assisted by means of *aids* from the rider's body, legs, and hands, to carry out the required actions.

The purpose of schooling is to make it easy for the horse to move well under the rider, and to help him to develop physically and mentally. We never seek to make the horse do anything unnatural; all we try to do is to cultivate Nature and to tame her.

Handling and Training

Gently Does It

By nature the horse is a timid creature whose main defence in the face of danger is to turn tail and run. Being ill equipped for a fight, he is rarely aggressive, and unless he discovers it by accident, he will remain ignorant of the potential he has for using his vastly superior strength against us. That said, however, many individuals are naturally dominant, and will not be made to do things against their will if they can avoid it.

Unless he is taught to respect his handler, the horse will soon have the upper hand and become unmanageable. He must always be handled firmly, but kindly and fairly. If he is treated roughly, or forced to do things for which he is ill prepared, or that are too difficult, then he may defy his trainer. He is bound to win any argument that descends to the level of a test of strength. The wise trainer will never let such a situation develop, for it would sour the relationship between man and horse, making further training very difficult.

Early Days

At no time is handling more important then during the initial stage of training, when the young horse is first introduced to school work. Unfortunately this

Horses must be treated firmly but gently or they will use their strength against us and may become dangerous.

Handling and Training (cont.)

period is commonly known as 'breaking in'. Such a phrase may describe the work of a horse dealer who wants to make a young horse ridable in a short space of time so he can turn a quick profit; but in no way does it express the gentleness with which the classical trainer will gradually accustom the horse to his new lifestyle. The horse's trust must be gained. His spirit must not be broken. He should be treated like an unschooled child, not as an enemy.

Generally, once the horse has accepted his rider's authority, he is an obliging partner who is ever willing to cooperate. It has been known for hundreds of years that forceful methods are out of place in the riding school, and furthermore that they do not yield the desired results.

Educating the Horse and Rider

Ignorant riders will use often use force as a last resort when they reach the limits of their knowledge and results are getting elusive. A true horseman when faced with a schooling problem will not act rashly, but will analyse the situation and devise a plan of action, or seek advice from a more experienced rider if necessary.

Training consists of educating the horse and helping him to move correctly. The process has to be slow and methodical so that he will get stronger

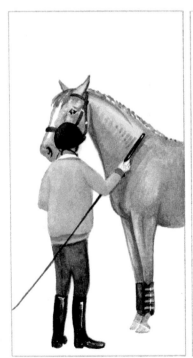

Take time to introduce the horse to unfamiliar equipment. He must learn to accept everything calmly without becoming anxious.

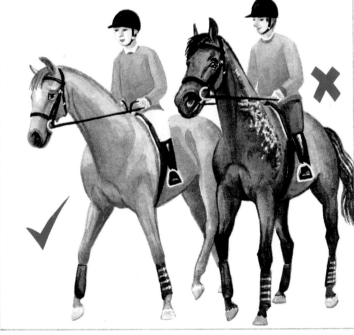

The horse must enjoy his education. He should be cool and calm after a training session, and should never be overworked.

by degrees without suffering stress or injury. Then he will be able to perform strenuous exercises without difficulty. If the training is hurried or if the horse is overworked there is a danger that he may get resentful, and he could even suffer physical and mental damage.

It takes three or four years for an expert to train a horse, but it can take ten or more years of learning and practice to become a good rider, and several more besides, to acquire the skills that are needed to train horses. This time is well spent, because there is more pleasure to be had in learning to master the skills of riding and in establishing a rapport with another living creature than there is in merely riding a finished horse that somebody else has trained.

Accomplished riders can control their mounts chiefly by the effects of their seat and legs, and to a lesser extent their hands. They use a minimum of equipment, and employ a bridle with a mild bit. They can expect their horses to improve gradually with time.

Poor riders use more severe bits and all sorts of auxiliary equipment which increase their physical dominance over the horse and help to compensate for their own weaknesses. Whilst such riders may gain some control, they inadvertently spoil the quality of the paces, and in time the horse will gradually deteriorate and become less pleasant to ride.

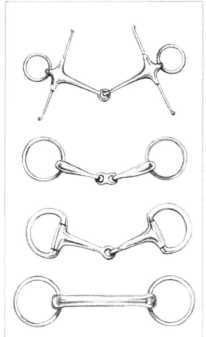

A simple snaffle is best for schooling. When correctly fitted it is comfortable for the horse, and its effects are mild.

Draw reins should not be used. They can do a lot of harm and spoil the horse because they force him to adopt an unnatural posture.

Relaxation

Moving without Tension

If a horse is to be attentive to his rider and move with smooth comfortable paces, he must be relaxed both mentally and physically. By physical relaxation we do not imply that he should be flabby and dull, but rather that he should not be tense or resistant. The horse must be fit, and he needs muscular strength so that he can carry out his work without tiring.

A tense horse may try to exercise his own will and comply only reluctantly with his rider's wishes. He will certainly be less responsive than the relaxed horse, who is receptive to the aids, and attendant to his rider's pleasure.

When there is tension, it must be eliminated by removing the cause. Sometimes this is badly fitting tack which hurts. Sometimes it is imperfect riding which causes the horse to tighten up in an attempt to protect himself from the discomfort. The horse has a good memory, and he is also a creature of habit; if he has suffered from a bad rider in the past he may become tense in anticipation of another unhappy experience.

The horse has no particular desire to expend muscular effort at our direction, and sometimes he will stiffen up deliberately as a means of resisting our aids and avoiding the work.

Calming the Horse

A tense horse can often be calmed by stroking his neck, by yielding the reins, and by talking to him in a soothing voice. Conversely, over-shortening or pulling on the reins will likely make him more tense, so such actions should not be contemplated.

A free walk on a long rein will settle an agitated horse. It will help the rider to relax too.

The free trot and free canter can be used to check just how relaxed the horse really is. When the reins are gradually lengthened, he should stretch his head and neck forwards and down. It is a sign of tension if the horse does not react in this way. This test can be applied to all horses, from the green youngster to the advanced school horse.

Any schooling done on a tense resistant horse will be unproductive. Relaxation should be established before other schooling objectives are pursued.

The simple act of stroking the horse's crest with one hand can induce relaxation very quickly.

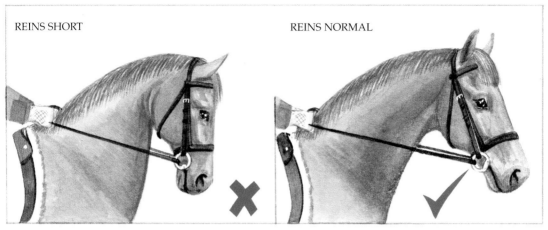

REINS SHORT

REINS NORMAL

If the rider holds the horse tightly the animal will not be able to relax. The reins must not constrain the horse, but must allow him to stretch his neck forwards.

The correct length of rein is neither more nor less than the distance between bit and hand when the horse is in a natural comfortable posture.

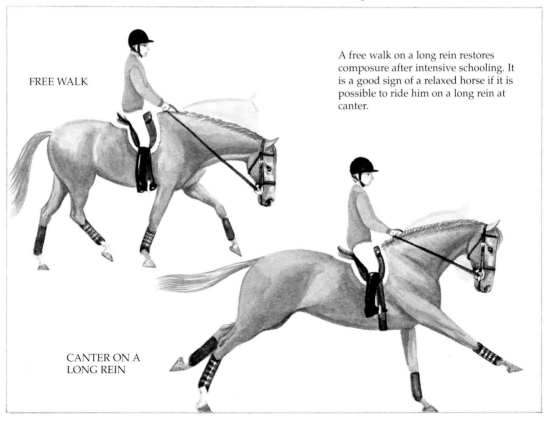

FREE WALK

A free walk on a long rein restores composure after intensive schooling. It is a good sign of a relaxed horse if it is possible to ride him on a long rein at canter.

CANTER ON A LONG REIN

Balance

The term 'balance' is used in horse riding to describe how well the horse moves about, and changes direction and speed whilst carrying the extra weight of a rider.

Weight Distribution

When young horses are first ridden, they often have difficulty finding their balance. They frequently change the distribution of weight over the forehand and the hindquarters.

Once horses become accustomed to carrying a rider they can balance themselves more easily. Then the proportion of weight borne by the front and hind limbs stays constant, and the head and neck remain steady.

Horses that are lazy with their hindlegs and prefer to carry more weight on their shoulders are said to be 'on the forehand', and they are always poorly balanced. They are inclined to run faster and faster as they move, and they can be quite hard to stop.

Well-balanced horses can be slowed down and stopped easily even if they are travelling at speed. They can maintain any desired pace with only a light contact on the bit, and the rider will not need to check the speed.

When changing direction unbalanced horses lean their shoulders into the turn and move in an ungainly manner, allowing their own momentum to carry them along. Balanced horses remain upright and in full control of their speed.

Tension and stiffness are prime destroyers of balance; if more time is spent helping the horse to relax, the balance will often improve automatically.

An unbalanced horse moves his head and neck about as he redistributes his weight. The gaits may become irregular and contact with the bit may be inconsistent.

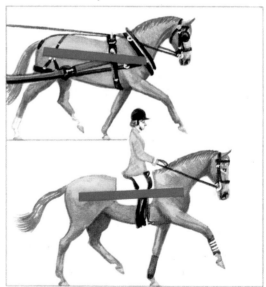

A horse's balance depends on how he supports his weight. Carriage horses take the weight on the shoulders. Riding horses must take the weight on the haunches.

10

The Half Halt

There are many exercises that can be used to help the horse to improve his balance by taking the weight back onto his haunches. One of the most important of these is called the *half halt*.

When the horse slows down or comes to a standstill in a proper manner, he does so by bending the joints of his hindlegs a little more so that they stop propelling him forwards, and support the weight instead. Thus if we practise halts we give the horse some exercise in a rebalancing activity.

The full halt is rather inconvenient to ride because it interrupts the flow of the movement. For this reason the half halt is generally employed instead. Here the rider begins to ask the horse to halt, but as soon as the latter has adjusted his balance in preparation, the rider allows him to move on again. The movement which follows the half halt invariably shows much better balance.

Nowadays the term 'half halt' is often applied to almost imperceptible balance adjustments which do not take the horse half way down to a halt.

Longer and Shorter Strides

Lengthening and shortening the stride is another very useful exercise for improving the balance. When asking for shorter strides the rider must not take up a stronger contact to slow the horse down, as that would prevent him from bending the joints of his hindlegs. The rider must adjust his seat to encourage more lift and less ground coverage in the stride and must use his legs to keep the horse's hindlegs stepping well forwards.

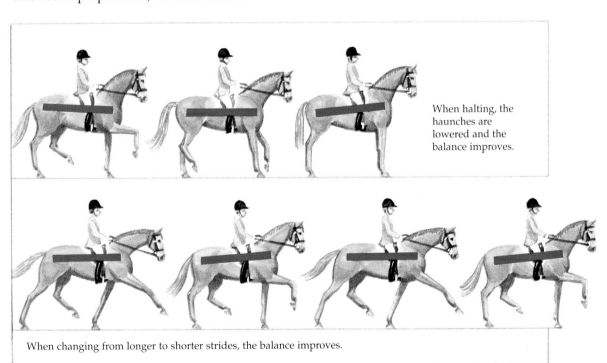

When halting, the haunches are lowered and the balance improves.

When changing from longer to shorter strides, the balance improves.

Balance (cont.)

Turns and Circles

Work on turns and circles is excellent for strengthening the hind limbs, because through the turns the inside hindleg is obliged to bend and carry more weight.

Lateral Movements

The so-called **lateral** exercises were devised centuries ago for making the horse more supple and for strengthening his hindquarters so that he would be able more easily to carry weight on his haunches. They are even more effective in improving the balance than work on turns and circles, but the horse needs a good basic education before he can be expected to attempt them.

In the **shoulder-in**, the rider bends his horse and brings his shoulders in from the track so that his inside hindleg is directed towards the centre of gravity, and is therefore obliged to lift and propel more weight than usual. This gymnastic exercise helps to strengthen the inside hock.

In the **haunches-in**, the rider brings the hindquarters in from the track so that the outside hindleg is positioned behind the centre of gravity. Here the horse's outside stifle joint gets the exercise.

In the **half-pass** the horse moves diagonally forwards and sideways, and is bent slightly towards the direction in which he is going. He crosses his outside hindleg over in front of his inside hindleg, and in so doing exercises the hip joint of the outer limb.

When all three lateral movements are practised in both directions, all the major joints of the hindlegs are exercised, and the muscles are strengthened. The horse's balance is sure to improve.

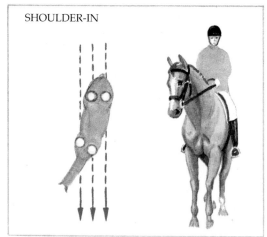

SHOULDER-IN

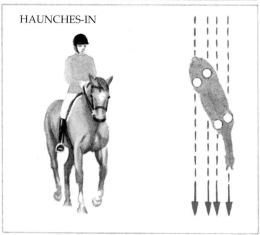

HAUNCHES-IN

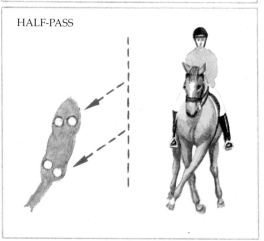

HALF-PASS

Regularity

Regular gaits give harmony to the experience of riding. Horses that are always changing rhythm are no fun to ride, and their paces look ugly too.

A Definition

Rhythmic regularity is achieved when the time interval between the start of each stride and the next remains constant.

The rhythm should not vary when the horse changes speed in the same gait. When going 'faster', he should take longer strides in the same rhythm, and not move his legs more rapidly. When going 'slower' he should take shorter higher steps without moving his limbs more slowly.

Increasing the tempo is a common evasion: the horse uses it to avoid the extra work required of the hindlegs.

A slow tempo is preferable because it encourages the horse to swing his back and exercise his whole body. When moving this way he is more responsive to the aids. The slow horse is also more attractive to watch in motion.

Controlling the Rhythm

When a horse moves irregularly it often indicates that his balance is not very good. More time must be spent on this aspect of his education.

When asking the horse to lengthen or shorten his strides, the rider should be sure that the rhythmic motion of his own body does not change as he swings along with the horse. This task will not be possible if his seat is disturbed by the motion of the horse, so a good seat is a very important asset.

If the horse tries to increase the tempo the rider can restore the rhythm by means of a half halt.

RUSHING: Quick, short steps

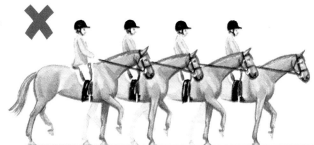

IN RHYTHM: Increasing speed

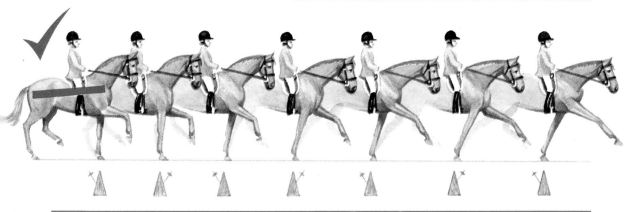

Energy and Impulsion

The Right Energy Level

For the horse to be easily ridable he must have enough energy that he can move willingly without the rider needing to egg him on continually. On the other hand he must not have so much energy that he rushes ahead obliging the rider to hold him back all the time. When the rider wants his horse to go faster he must be able to achieve this result by increasing the driving aids, rather than by diminishing the effect of the stopping aids.

Willingness to move forwards is a basic instinct in the horse, and every animal has his own particular level of energy output. One of the reasons that warmbloods are a popular choice for riders wishing to specialise in dressage is that their natural energy level renders them easy to train and pleasant to ride.

The rider has some influence over the amount of energy that the horse produces. For example, he can energise the horse and improve his responsiveness by practising frequent transitions.

The Unwilling Horse

If the horse finds moving about uncomfortable, then he will not be very keen to move, and may resist the rider's aids. The rider must be easy for him to carry, so it is important to be able to accommodate the motion of the horse's back smoothly without bumping about in the saddle.

The Fresh Horse

An abundance of energy can be caused by a natural exuberance which has never been contained, too much energising feed, or lack of exercise. All these things are under the rider's control. It can also be due to temporary excitement aroused

LAZY

Horses with too little or too much energy present difficulties for the rider. They are easy to ride when the energy output is just right.

BUCKING

MOVING WELL UNDER CONTROL

by prevailing conditions. Skilful and sensitive handling will be required.

Creating Impulsion

Controlled energy combined with strength and power is generally referred to as *impulsion.*

If a harnessed draught horse is prevented from moving forwards he will mark time on the spot. His great strength gives him much impulsion.

A racehorse has plenty of energy but it is all released as speed, and not controlled in the same sense. There is a wise saying that 'speed is the enemy of impulsion'.

A poorly balanced horse that runs when he is asked to lengthen his stride has energy, but not impulsion. This horse would not be able canter straight from a walk; he would have to get up speed in trot first. By contrast, a horse with a great deal of impulsion would easily be able to glide into a canter directly from a standstill.

To move with impulsion, the horse needs physical strength in his hind legs, and in his topline, in addition to a suitable level of energy output. It is impossible to develop impulsion unless the horse is relaxed, balanced, and capable of maintaining regular gaits in good rhythm.

Without impulsion the horse would be unable to perform any advanced school movements. The rider should always try to develop impulsion and must be careful not to allow the horse to squander his energies as speed.

SPEED

IMPULSION

PASSAGE

To perform a passage the horse needs impulsion – a slow, controlled release of energy. An impatient draught horse has more impulsion than a racehorse.

Bending and Suppleness

From the rider's point of view a supple horse is a joy to ride, whereas a stiff one has rough jolting movements and can be very uncomfortable. From the horse's standpoint, a stiff rider is an unwelcome passenger, whilst a supple one enables him to move comfortably.

Poor riding can lead to stiffness in the horse, but this is not the only cause. Lack of suitable equine gymnastic exercise will leave some muscles under-used, and some joints will never really get loosened up. Some form of regular schooling is indispensable if the horse is to be kept supple.

Suppleness can be much improved by practising bending exercises. There is nothing to match these for their ability to stretch muscles and flex joints.

The horse can bend not only *laterally* to left and right, such as when he is ridden through turns, but also *longitudinally*, such as when he is asked to lengthen or shorten his strides. When schooling, it is a good idea to alternate between lateral and longitudinal bending exercises.

Lateral Bending

Numerous patterns are available to the trainer who wishes to bend his horse laterally. The circle, the spiral, the serpentine, and the figure-of-eight are good examples. The lateral movements are also very helpful.

The amount of lateral bending that the horse can show is dependent on his stage of training. Young horses cannot manage tight turns or small circles: if the rider were to attempt too tight a turn then nothing would be gained, because either the horse would take short steps and lose the rhythm, or he would move crookedly.

There is an absolute limit to the amount of lateral bending that is achievable as a result of training. The volte is the smallest circle that the advanced horse is asked to negotiate. This is a circle whose radius is equal to the horse's length.

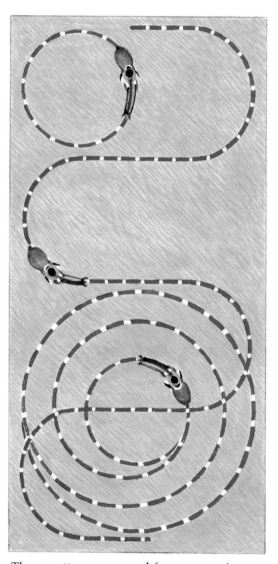

These patterns are good for encouraging lateral bending and making the horse supple.

Longitudinal Bending

Longitudinal bending exercises give the horse a chance to stretch his body, and they allow him to swing his back; they flex and stretch the joints of his hindlegs, and they help to transfer weight back towards his haunches.

There are two main types of exercise. In the first the gait is unchanged but the horse is allowed to stretch his frame by lowering his head and neck as the rider yields the reins. This can be done at walk, trot, or canter, and when riding any pattern, including the lateral movements.

In the second the horse's frame is kept substantially the same, but he is asked to lengthen and shorten his strides. This can be practised on any pattern or lateral movement too.

As the training progresses the horse will gradually extend the limits of his lengthening and shortening.

The rein-back, and direct transitions, such as trot to halt, and walk to canter also exercise the horse longitudinally.

Suppleness is closely related to strength. The supple horse is able to perform more difficult exercises, which in turn help to build up his musculature.

Provided the rider is mindful of the basic principles of schooling, works his horse equally on both reins, and is careful to increase his demands gradually, he should automatically produce a horse that is loose and supple. Suppleness is a good measure of the success of the schooling.

HALT TO TROT

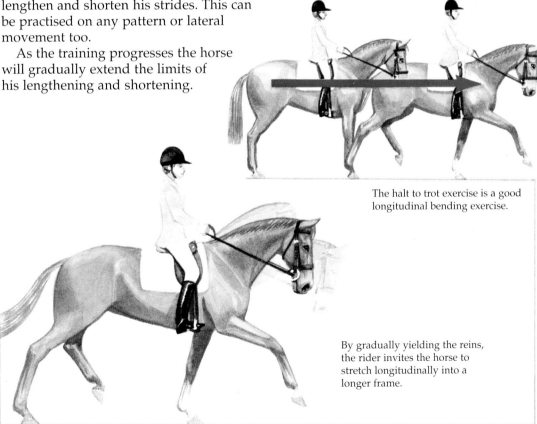

The halt to trot exercise is a good longitudinal bending exercise.

By gradually yielding the reins, the rider invites the horse to stretch longitudinally into a longer frame.

Straightness

Natural Crookedness

Like us, horses are rarely ambidextrous. They find it easier to bend and turn in one direction. They usually load their hind limbs unevenly, favouring one more than the other, so that their hindquarters deviate to one side and they become crooked.

Crookedness causes all sorts of problems with horses:

- the contact with the bit is firm on one side and soft on the other
- they lean towards one shoulder
- they cut corners to avoid loading the weaker hindleg
- they have a preferred leading leg at canter
- they perform the lateral movements quite differently in either direction.

Straightening the Horse

The rider must be careful to keep the horse's shoulders in line with his hindquarters, and must not allow him to lean on the rein on the side with the stronger contact.

Many exercises can be used to help the horse to develop both sides evenly so that any crookedness diminishes. Bending exercises are particularly effective. It is a well known fact that without bending, straightness cannot be obtained.

Lateral movements can be chosen to work particular joints in the hindlegs that the rider feels are weak. The strike-off into canter can also be used to strengthen a weak hindleg. A transition into a right lead canter, for example, will help to strengthen the left hindleg.

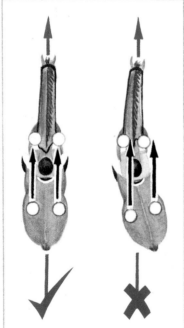

To be straight the horse's hind feet must follow in the tracks made by his forefeet, and not step out to one side.

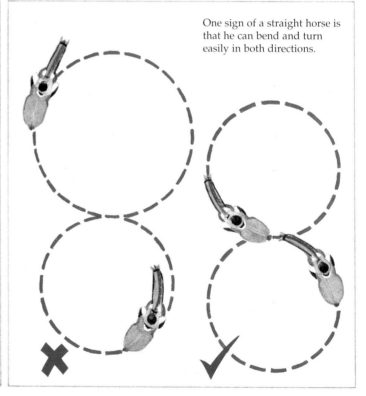

One sign of a straight horse is that he can bend and turn easily in both directions.

18

Contact

Lightness and Consistency

In keeping with the principle that the horse performs best when he is relaxed and free from constraint, the contact between the rider's hand and the horse's mouth should be kept very light. Pressure on the reins should be no more than a few ounces.

It would not be possible to train a horse with no contact at all, because then there would be no way to persuade him to take more weight onto his haunches. Some contact is essential, to define the limit to which the horse is allowed to stretch, and to provide a fixed point of reference up to which the hindlegs can be advanced.

Taking weight onto the haunches involves extra muscular activity, which like all living things, the horse will avoid if he possibly can. With a loose rein he could, and would, deliberately evade the engaging effects of the rider's seat and legs.

If the rider succeeds in engaging the haunches, the horse's balance will improve, and he will raise his head and neck, causing the rein contact to lighten, and providing an opportunity for the rider to work on a slightly shorter rein. With just the right amount of engaging activity from the rider, a light contact can always be maintained.

The rider must at all times provide a consistent contact. This can only be done if the seat is good and the hands can be kept absolutely still relative to the horse. Riders who are unable to provide such a contact can usually produce a better result by resting their hands down on the front of the saddle or on their thighs. This stabilises the hands and provides the horse with a passive bit to contact.

REINS TOO LOOSE

TOO TIGHT

GOOD CONTROL

EXTRA STABILITY

Contact (cont.)

Positioning the Head

The horse must be given a light but definite contact, so that his head is not confined by the reins, and its position can indicate how he is distributing his body weight.

If the horse does not carry his head in a good position the reins must not be used to lift it or to hold it in the proper place. The correction must be made by driving the hindlegs further forwards so that the weight is taken back. Then the horse will raise his forehand and automatically adopt a better position.

If there is any appreciable pressure on the bit then the reins are probably being held too short for the horse's current state of balance. If the reins hang loose then they are too long, and the horse will remain uncollected and not fully under control.

In nature the horse uses his head and neck as a counterbalancing weight, and if the rider interferes with this by putting tension on the reins, it makes it very difficult for the horse to move well. Pressure on the reins has an indirect effect on the hindlegs: it impedes their free forward movement, which is counter-productive.

Seeking a Contact

A fundamental rule is that the horse must seek a contact with the bit. When the rider yields the reins, the horse must stretch his nose forwards and down in an attempt to recontact the bit. The rider has no business in shortening the reins to contact the horse's mouth: it is the horse's job to contact the bit, and the rider's job to teach the horse to do this.

With a light contact the hindlegs step freely forwards.

A strong contact restricts the action of the hindlegs.

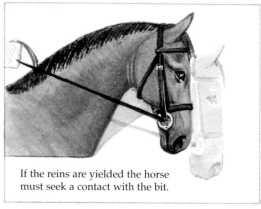

If the reins are yielded the horse must seek a contact with the bit.

Self-Carriage

As the horse's training progresses, he will learn to move more in 'self-carriage'. This means that he will be strong enough to support the weight of his own head and neck in a good posture without tiring and without depending on the reins for support.

The rider can test for self-carriage by releasing the reins and seeing for how long the horse can hold his position.

Turning and Stopping

Although the reins do play a part in turning the horse and in making him stop, it would be very wrong to pull on them to achieve either of these objectives. A horse that is compelled to act by forceful means will never move willingly or gracefully, and will develop harsh uncomfortable movements.

When turning or circling, the horse must bend his body towards the direction of the turn, and take more weight on his inside hindleg.

The reins can be used in conjunction with the rider's seat and legs to help the horse to turn, in the following way: the inside rein remains passive, its function being to indicate the direction of the bend. The outside rein yields, allowing the horse to stretch forwards on that side, and turn in the required direction. By limiting the amount of yielding the rider controls the degree to which the horse is able to bend, and hence the size of the turn that he will make.

When a horse will not bend easily, an exaggerated yielding of the outside rein may help. With a well-schooled horse, however, the rider's inside leg causes the inside hock to flex, and the inside hindleg supports the weight, enabling the horse to adopt a curved posture. There is then no need to emphasise the yielding of the outside rein. The rider can hold this rein steady, and the horse will take a lighter contact on the inside rein.

TURNING

STOPPING

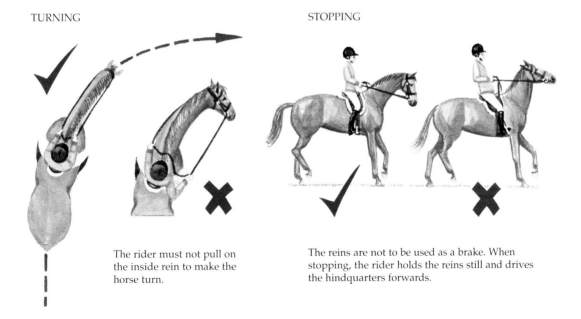

The rider must not pull on the inside rein to make the horse turn.

The reins are not to be used as a brake. When stopping, the rider holds the reins still and drives the hindquarters forwards.

Collection

The collected horse is responsive and obedient. His energies are concentrated, so that he is ready to perform immediately and effortlessly, whatever his rider may ask him to do.

What is Collection?

In a sense collection is the ultimate objective of riding because it embodies all the qualities that are desirable in the riding horse. It renders the horse particularly pleasant to ride, and it can sometimes impart to the rider the sensation that he and his horse are merged together to form a single creature that thinks and moves as one.

The essence of collection is that the horse carries more weight on his haunches. Hence it is closely related to, and dependent on balance.

The demeanour of the hindquarters is affected by an increased bending of the hock, stifle, and hip joints, and by a tilting of the pelvis which increases the roundness of the horse's lower back. The croup is slightly lowered and the forehand somewhat raised.

In profile the horse appears more compact. His neck arches attractively and his poll flexes, so that the line of his face approaches the vertical. He takes shorter but loftier steps, which are said to be *cadenced*. His body is supple, and he treads softly upon the ground.

Obtaining Collection

All the principles of schooling must be put into practice if collection is to be obtained. The horse must be relaxed and balanced, move straight with regularity and impulsion, and take an even contact on both sides of the bit.

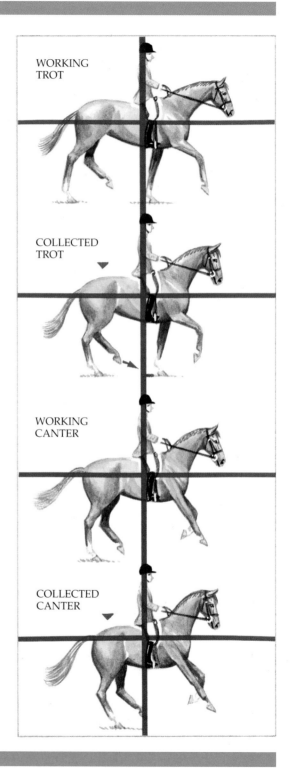

WORKING TROT

COLLECTED TROT

WORKING CANTER

COLLECTED CANTER

Aids for Collection

Collection does not come easily. Some riders try to achieve it by pulling back on the reins and shortening the horse from the front. This is never successful; it causes tension, and destroys lightness in the forehand. There are no short cuts to producing that characteristic posture of collection which is so desirable.

Whilst offering a non-yielding contact to prevent speeding up or lengthening, the rider uses his seat and legs to ask the horse to bend his joints and carry more weight on the haunches. All the aids relax as the horse responds.

The Limits of Collection

Maximum collection at the trot produces the 'piaffe', where the horse marks time on the spot. At canter the horse can execute a 'pirouette', a 360° turn.

Because the walk has less natural impulsion than the either the trot or the canter a good collected walk is very difficult to produce. It is available only to dedicated students of riding.

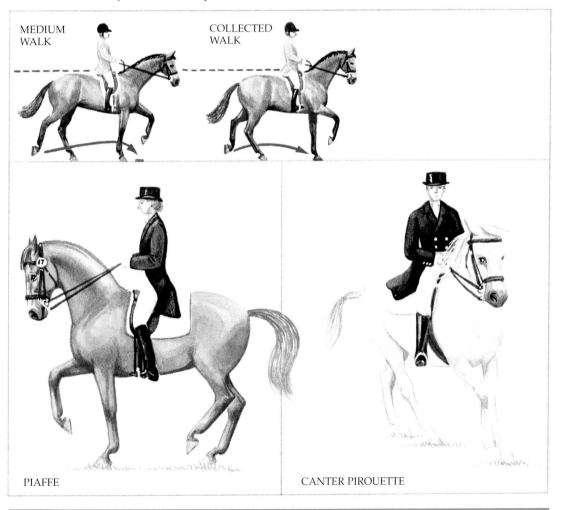

MEDIUM WALK

COLLECTED WALK

PIAFFE

CANTER PIROUETTE

Three Stages of Training

Classical training is made up of three separate stages or schools. The first two are for all riding horses. The third is for those specialising in advanced dressage.

Riding Straight Forward
The first stage usually begins in the young horse's fourth year, and lasts for a period of one year.

Ridden work does not begin until the horse is calm, obedient, and moving correctly on the lunge. Exercise consists of work on straight lines and large simple patterns. The main objectives are to get the horse obedient to the aids, calm, active, straight in his action, and physically fit enough for the demands of the next stage.

Campaign School
An experienced trainer would be able to get most horses through this stage in a year or two. Most horse owners would need more time than this.

Work includes riding the collected horse around small circles and short turns, the lateral movements, direct transitions, and flying changes.

The main objective is to produce a versatile riding horse that is easy and pleasant to ride.

High school, or 'Haute école'
High school riding transgresses the functional, and approaches the realms of art. It includes some spectacular movements that are rather fun to ride.

This stage would be unthinkable without a comprehensive basic education: the horse must be very thoroughly trained.

High school movements are divided into 'airs on the ground', and 'airs above the ground'. The airs on the ground include all the difficult exercises that have to be shown in Grand Prix dressage tests: the piaffe, the passage, the canter pirouette, and sequences of flying changes.

Airs above the ground are so called because the horse raises both his fore feet from the ground. Only a few very exceptional horses can do them.

Horses are trained only for airs that they show a natural inclination to perform. In the *capriole,* shown below, the horse jumps up in the air and kicks out his heels at the height of the leap.